Exploding Gravy

X. J. KENNEDY

Exploding Gravy

Poems to Make You Laugh

Illustrated by Joy Allen

Little, Brown and Company
Boston New York London

Also by X. J. Kennedy
(and Dorothy M. Kennedy):

Knock at a Star
Talking Like the Rain

First Edition

Some of the poems in this collection have appeared in *One Winter Night in August; The Phantom Ice Cream Man; Ghastlies, Goops and Pincushions;* and *Uncle Switch,* all published by Margaret K. McElderry Books, and *Did Adam Name the Vinegarroon?,* published by David R. Godine.

Some of the poems previously uncollected first appeared in *The Big Book for Our Planet,* edited by Ann Durrell, Jean Craighead George, and Katherine Paterson (Dutton Children's Books, 1993); *The 20th Century Children's Poetry Treasury,* selected by Jack Prelutsky (Alfred A. Knopf, 1999); and *Light, the Quarterly of Light Verse.*

Library of Congress Cataloging-in-Publication Data

Kennedy, X. J.
   Exploding Gravy : poems to make you laugh / by X. J. Kennedy ; illustrated by Joy Allen.– 1st ed.
   p. cm.
   Includes index.
   ISBN 0-316-38423-2
   1. Children's poetry, American. 2. Humorous poetry, American. [1. Humorous poetry. 2. American poetry.] I. Allen, Joy, ill. II. Title.
   PS3521.E563 E88 2002
   811'.54– dc21   2001029282

10 9 8 7 6 5 4 3 2 1

RRD - IN

Printed in the United States of America

To You

If through this book
   You go on reading,
Take a good look.
   No need for speeding.

Contents

1

Far-Out Families

Mother's Nerves

My mother said, "If just once more
I hear you slam that old screen door,
I'll tear out my hair!
I'll dive in the stove!"
So I gave it a bang and in she dove.

Backyard Volcano

Why oh why did an active volcano
　　Have to poke up its nose in our yard?
It goes *gloop* like a sink full of Drano
　　And it showers down rocks that hit hard.

From its crest you can gaze upon masses
　　Of boulders that bubble and seethe,
And it's giving off ghastly green gases
　　That nobody's able to breathe.

"Balls of fire!" Uncle Jack yells, jackknifing
　　Down into that smoldering cone,
"What a fine, steamy day to go diving!
　　Last one in is an old molten stone!"

Now each night, with a cup of hot java,
　　Mother props up her feet, feeling snug
While she watches red rivers of lava
　　Roll over our living-room rug.

3

Father and Mother

My father's name is Frankenstein,
He comes from the Barbados.
He fashioned me from package twine
And instant mashed potatoes.

My mother's name is Draculeen,
She lets a big bat bite her,
And folks who sleep here overnight
Wake up a few quarts lighter.

Guinevere Ghastly
Sits Baby

"Guinevere, where's brother Peter?"

"Tied fast to the parking meter.
Don't worry, Mom. I stuck a dime
Down him. He's still got lots of time."

Alarm

Mother come quick!
Robert looks sick!
He opened the shoe polish, took a big lick!

His face is all weird!
He's grown a brown beard!
All four walls, the floor, and the ceiling are
     smeared!

Come look and see!
Don't you wish he
Was never a trouble to people, like me?

Great-Great Grandma, Don't Sleep in Your Treehouse Tonight

Great-Great Grandma, don't sleep in your
    treehouse tonight,
    Don't swing on your rope and your tire,
'Cause your tree felt the bite
Of a mighty termite.
        Have a seat
        By the heat
    Of the fire.

Here's a big bowl of black
Bolts and nuts you can crack,
    Here's some cider to slide down your craw.
        Oh, what fun it'll be
        When we roast that old tree —
            None so tall
            Stands in all
Arkansas!

7

Help!

Firemen, firemen!
State police!
Victor's locked in Pop's valise!
Robert's eating Kitty Litter!
Doctor!
   Lawyer!
      Baby-sitter!

A Social Mixer

Father said, "Heh, heh! I'll fix her!" —
Threw Mother in the concrete mixer.

She whirled about and called, "Come hither!"
It looked like fun, so he jumped in with her.

Then in to join that dizzy dance
Jumped Auntie Bea and Uncle Anse.

In leaped my little sister Lena
And Chuckling Chuck, her pet hyena.

Even Granmaw Fanshaw felt a yearning
To do some high-speed overturning.

All shouted through the motor's whine,
"Aw come on in — the concrete's fine!"

I jumped in too and got all scrambly.
Isn't ours a mixed-up family?

Making Light of Auntie

I like to shuffle in my socks
   Across our scuffy carpet
And touch Aunt Sue and give her shocks.
   I gave her one so sharp it
Caused her to shoot out of her shoes
   With — wow! — a big blue spark.
Now Auntie Sue's the bulb we use
   To read by after dark.

The Vacuum Cleaner's
Swallowed Will

The vacuum cleaner's swallowed Will.
   He's vanished. What a drag.
Still, we can do without him till
   It's time to change the bag.

Long-Distance Call

Babbling baby, left alone,
Punched some buttons on the phone.

Poppa paid for her to coo
All the way to Katmandu.

In the Motel

Bouncing, bouncing on the beds,
Brother Bob and I cracked heads —

People next door heard that CRACK,
Whammed on the wall, so we whammed
 right back.

Dad's razor caused an overload
And wow! did the TV set explode!

Someone's car backed up and—tinkle!
In our windshield was a wrinkle.

Eight more days on the road? Hooray!
What a bang-up holiday!

The Cat Who Aspired to Higher Things

Our cat turns up her nose at mice.
She thinks rhinoceroses
Are twice as nice as mice to chase,
But now the mice are everyplace —

In the furnace,
In the freezer,
In Aunt Edith's orange squeezer,

In the cellar,
In the cider,
In Great-Grandpa's best hang glider,

In the ginger,
In the allspice,
In Aunt Flora's King Kong false face,

In the stamps,
In the chocolate section
Of my ice-cream cone collection —

All four of my Uncle Erics
Tear their hair and throw hysterics.
Father smashes chairs and cusses.

At least we've no rhinoceroses.

Granddad's Rising

When Granddad goes to bed he hangs
His artificial hair
On a carpet tack stuck fast to the back
Of an old three-legged chair,

But when the roosters crow he gives
A whistle shrill and merry,
Grabs wig off the tack and claps it back
And once again he's hairy.

He gropes the floor for his loose glass eye
And plugs it in its socket,
Straps on his wooden leg again
And twists a key to lock it.

He grabs his false teeth from the glass
Where all night they've been sopping
And pokes 'em in where they belong.
Soon flapjacks he starts chopping.

It seems a piecemeal kind of thing,
The way his new day starts.
Oh, how in the world can Granddad be
The sum of all those parts?

17

Mother, a Dog Is at the Door

Mother, a dog is at the door
Demanding your moleskin hat!
   No, daughter my child, it drives dogs wild.
   We don't dare give him that.

Mother, he said he'd take instead
Your billy goat's old canoe.
   Good gracious, no! That isn't to go,
   It's stuck fast with airplane glue.

Mother, he'd trade some lemonade
For your bicycle-pumpkin pie.
   Oh, would he, the bum? If I lost one crumb
   Of that delicate stuff, I'd die!

Mother, I'm scared! He's all bristly-haired!
He's foaming like canned whipped-cream!
Tell him, my dear, that indeed I fear
I shall stand on my head and scream.

Oh, Mother, he's peeling his teeth away!
It's Father in dog's disguise!
Why, daughter my own, I ought to have known
That a dog wouldn't want my pies.

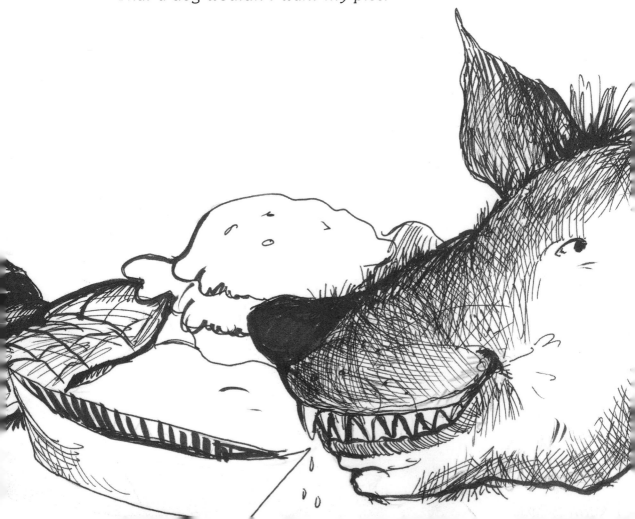

A Day of Play

Said the mom of the baby blue shark,
"Try the beach at the national park.
    You'll have wonderful fun
    Making everyone run—
Just be sure, dear, you're home before dark."

2

Witches, Ghosts, Dragons, & Monsters

Wicked Witch's Kitchen

You're in the mood for freaky food?
You feel your taste buds itchin'
For nice fresh poison ivy greens?
Try Wicked Witch's kitchen!

She has corn on the cobweb, cauldron-hot,
She makes the meanest cider,
But her broomstick cakes and milkweed shakes
Aren't fit to feed a spider.

She likes to brew hot toadstool stew —
"Come eat, my sweet!" she'll cackle —
But if you do, you'll turn into
A jack-o'-lantern's jackal.

22

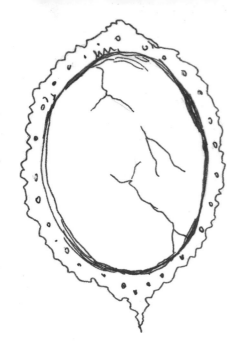

Wicked Witch Admires Herself

"Mirror, mirror on the wall,
Whose is the fairest face of all?
I'll come close, so you'll see me clearer —"

CRACK! goes another magic mirror.

A Bright Spirit

Every Hallowe'en, Ghostly McGrew
Sticks his skull to his neck with a screw
   And he washes his thorax
   In buckets of borax
Until it looks shiny as new.

Whose Boo Is Whose?

Two ghosts I know once traded heads
And shrieked and shook their sheets to shreds —
"You're me!" yelled one, "and me, I'm you!
Now who can boo the loudest boo?"

"Me!" cried the other, and for proof
He booed a boo that scared the roof
Right off our house. Our TV set
Jumped higher than a jumbo jet.

The first ghost snickered, "Why, you creep,
Call that a boo? That feeble beep?
Hear this!" — and sucking in a blast
Of wind, he puffed his sheet so vast

And booed so hard, a passing goose
Lost all its down. The moon came loose
And fell and smashed to smithereens.
Stars scattered like spilled jelly beans.

"How's that for booing, boy? I win!"
Said one. The other scratched a chin
Where only bone was — "Win or lose?
How can we tell whose boo is whose?"

The Skeleton Walks

Right after our Thanksgiving feast
Our turkey's bones went hobblin'
To Joan the wicked witch's house
To be her turkey goblin.

My Dragon

I have a purple dragon with
A long brass tail that clangs,
And anyone not nice to me
Soon feels his fiery fangs.

So if you tell me I'm a dope
Or call my muscles jelly,
You just might dwell a million years
Inside his boiling belly.

Sir Percival and the Dragon

"Sir Percival,
Be merciful,"
    The cornered dragon begged.
"There'll never be
Another me
    So mean, so many-legged.

"What fiercer foe
Than I could show
    Your golden-headed charmer
How you don't cringe?
Who else so singe
    The brightness of your armor?

"Though kings hold sway
And swear they'll pay
    The knight who works my slaughter
Half some dull town,
An old half crown,
    And the hand of their cross-eyed
        daughter,

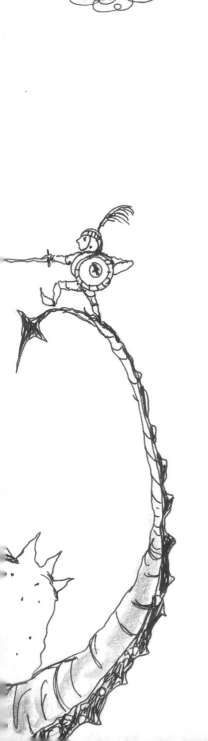

"For such reward
Why dent your sword?
　　Such deeds seem rash and reckless.
I guard the door
To gold galore —
　　Here, have a diamond necklace.

"Tell them at court
They may cavort:
　　The dragon they've been dreading
Is now done in.
Display my skin,
　　This old one I'm through shedding.

"Your blue eyes flash?
You seek not cash
　　But only fame and virtue?
Through dragon lore
Your name shall soar —
　　That's not to sneeze at. KER-choo!"

"Quite right! Why fight?"
Agreed the knight.
　　"I'll give you no more jabs, sir.
Go guard your hoard.
I'll save my sword
　　For broiling shish kebabs, sir."

The Abominable
Baseball Bat

I swung and swung at empty air
And when I heard the umpire
Behind me shout, "Strike three — you're out!"
My bat turned to a vampire.

The whole team had to pry it loose.
Poor Ump looked pale and flat.
Now ever since, my bat and I
Never strike out at bat.

The Phantom
Ice Cream Man

When frost unlocks the last stiff leaf
And autumn stars start twinkling,
The North Wind's wolf pack prowls our street.
On such nights I've an inkling

Of someone strange. I catch my breath
Between cold bedsheets, hearing
The far-off tingle of his bell,
Now faint, but slowly nearing . . .

Then why not raise the window shade
And look? Oh no, I daren't
For fear I'll see a man in white
On a truck dim and transparent.

He calls in sweetly wheedling tones,
Familiar, almost human,
"Frostsicles? Frozen-yogurt cones?
Who'll try my chocolate snowmen?"

Taste ice cream from another world
And you'll become a phantom,
Be seized by hands of breeze, be whirled
With dizzying momentum

To lands of everlasting ice
Where, captive in his castle,
Ringed round by hounds with fangs that freeze,
You'll try to move a muscle

And can't. Who'd buy such costly cones?
Yet his cry sets things to seeming:
Now old enchantments walk my room
And breathe. Can I be dreaming?

I smell mown clover's lost perfume,
Hear pigeons flute and murmur.
I hear once more the creaking board
That swung me through last summer —

   July alive!
   Then far away
And soft, his music hovers.
White winter drifts to earth. I draw
Head deep inside warm covers.

3

Eats

Snowflake
Soufflé

Snowflake soufflé
Snowflake soufflé
Makes a lip-smacking lunch
On an ice-cold day!

You take seven snowflakes,
You break seven eggs,
And you stir it seven times
With your two hind legs.

Bake it in an igloo,
Throw it on a plate,
And you slice off a slice
With a rusty ice skate.

36

Exploding Gravy

My mother's big green gravy boat
Once thought he was a navy boat.

I poured him over my mashed potatoes
And out swam seven swift torpedoes.

Torpedoes whizzed and whirred and—
     WHAM!
One bumped smack into my hunk of ham

And blew up with an awful roar,
Flinging my carrots on the floor.

Exploding gravy! That's so silly!
Now all I ever eat is chili.

My Birthday Cake
Is Acting Strange

My birthday cake is acting strange:
   It struts around on legs.
It sits on our electric range
   And lays milk chocolate eggs.

It's like a hen in lots of ways —
   It cackles, clucks, and scratches
And out of every egg it lays
   A little cupcake hatches.

Skunk Cabbage Slaw

Skunk cabbage slaw has one bad flaw —
It's tough to gnaw a jawful.
You chaw and chaw. It's rough when raw,
But cooked, it smells just awful.

Skunk cabbage slaw! Don't make it, Maw!
For weeks we've chomped and chomped,
But all these green and swamp-grown leaves
Leave (groan!) our stomachs swamped.

Italian Noodles

Whenever I
Eat ravioli
I fork it fast
And chew it sloli.

A meatballed mound
Of hot spaghetti—
To slurp it down
I'm always rhetti

And when it comes
To pipelike ziti,
I just don't know
A sight more priti.

Wouldn't you love
To have lasagna
Any old time
The mood was on ya?

Oh why oh why
Do plates of pasta
Make my heart start
Fluttering fasta?

Unusual Shoelaces

To lace my shoes
I use spaghetti.
Teachers and friends
All think I'm batty.

Let 'em laugh, the whole
Kit and kaboodle.
Oh, I'll get by.
I use my noodle.

A Choosy Wolf

"Why won't you eat me, wolf?" I asked.

"It wouldn't be much fun to.
Besides, I'm into natural foods
That nothing has been done to."

Kangaroo and Kiwi

A crazy kangaroo I knew
Who'd always giggle ("Tee-hee!")
Grabbed a big flat pie and let it fly
At a little peewee kiwi.

That kiwi, though, she ducked down low
And let that missile miss her.
It circled back and it landed — whack! —
In the kangaroo's own kisser.

Said kiwi, "My, that's tricky pie,
Must be a custard boomerang?"
"No," said kangaroo, smacking her lips,
"It's a lemon kangaroo-meringue."

Cocoa Skin Coat

If I had a coat
Made of cocoa skin
With marshmallow buttons
Right up to my chin,

I'd skip on my toes!
I'd skim on my tummy
In my cocoa skin coat
All warm and scummy!

4

Giants & Dinosaurs

Hickenthrift
and Hickenloop

Hickenthrift and Hickenloop
   Stood fourteen mountains high.
They'd wade the wind, they'd have to stoop
   To let the full moon by.

Their favorite sport, played on a court,
   Was called Kick Down the Castle —
They'd stamp their boots, those vast galoots,
   Till king lay low as vassal.

One day while spooning hot rock soup
   From a volcano crater,
Said Hickenthrift, "Say, Hickenloop,
   Which one of us is greater?"

Across the other's jagged brow
   Dark thunder seemed to drift
And Hickenloop, with one swift swoop,
   Ate straight through Hickenthrift.

47

The Up-to-Date Giant

I'm all caught up, I'm where things are!
   I've swapped my old self-strumming
Harp for an amplified guitar.
   No more fee-fi-fo-fumming.

I can't stand Englishmen's ground bones,
   They clog my cookie cutter,
And golden eggs taste — yuk! — like stones.
   Please pass the peanut butter.

Living on a Giant

Oh, we live in a house in the giant's left ear —
    We've a happy and friendly alliance.
In the woods of his whiskers our schoolhouse sits near.
    We do projects on giants for science.

When it's winter we break out our skates, sticks, and pucks.
    Both his eyeballs make wonderful rinks.
When it's summer we dive in and paddle like ducks —
    Just jump out of the way when he winks!

Woolly Mammoth

When glassy glaciers glided south
And ice was all the rage,
This great-grandpappy elephant
Wore wool to suit his Age.

A hairy mountain ten feet tall
With peepers moist and misty,
He stood as solid as a wall,
His twin tusks long and twisty.

By someone in Siberia
A bunch of these vast geezers
Were once discovered big as life
And fresh as fish in freezers.

The Trouble
with a Dinosaur

The trouble with a dinosaur
Is how to move while ambling
And how to sit and hatch her eggs
Without the whole bunch scrambling.

Tyrannosaurus Rex

A mean, late-model dinosaur,
  He walked Creation vastly.
His teeth were something to deplore;
  His table manners, ghastly.

With hungry jaws he laid harsh laws
  Upon the reptile nation.
By day and night his appetite
  Decreased its population.

But tyrants, under Time's slow hand,
  One day must bow their necks.
Now in museums — bones wired — stand
  Tyrannosaurus wrecks.

Dinosaur Din

Did stegosaurus bellow
Like a longhorn steer from Texas?
Could a bird's sweet tweet
Conceivably beat
Tyrannosaurus rex's?

Did pterodactyl cackle?
Did brachiosaurus bray?
Did monoclonious toot
Through his horny snoot
Ta ra ra boom de ay?

Did little lambeosaurus baa
In a big loud sheepish chorus?
Did the ankles clank
Like an army tank
Upon ankylosaurus?

Today, cars, planes, and subway trains
Make a hubbubish hullabaloo,
But the rumble and roar
Of a dinosaur
I never have heard. Have you?

55

Diplodocus Holiday

One night in a dark museum
When a dusty old clock struck ONE,
Two skeleton diplodocuses
Decided to have some fun,

Stepped stiffly off their pedestals
On ghostly toes all hazy
And grabbed two stegosaurus skulls
And bowled down bones like crazy.

They rock-and-rolled around the room,
They made showcases rattle,
They rode a dodo piggyback—
A fossil bawled, "I'll tattle!"

"It's too darned long now since we died,"
In voices thin as paper
Those diplodocus ghosts replied.
"High time we cut a caper!"

One seized a pterodactyl's tail
(Which didn't have much feeling)
And glided it and watched it bash
A hole right through the ceiling.

They munched some million-year-old eggs
Whose yokes were gray and musty.
"What yucky stuff!" one groaned. "I fear
At finding food we're rusty."

Then, hearing Will the Watchman's steps,
They gave two leaps and froze
Back on their own home pedestals
In innocent repose.

"I could have sworn —" said baffled Will,
But all looked quite all right
In that murky old museum room
In the middle of the night.

Longest Lizard

Diplodocus, the longest lizard,
With green leaves liked to fill his gizzard
And probably would not have taken
One single bite of steak or bacon
Or you or me, if we'd been current
Back then.
                But still, good thing we weren't.

5

Birds, Bees, & Beasts

Vulture

The vulture's very like a sack
   Set down and left there drooping:
His crooked beak and creaky back
   Look badly bent from stooping
Down to the ground to eat dead cows
   So they won't go to waste,
Thus making up in usefulness
   For what he lacks in taste.

Who to Pet
and Who Not To

Go pet a kitten, pet a dog,
Go pet a worm for practice,
But don't go pet a porcupine —
You want to be a cactus?

Powder Puff

The Whales Off Wales

With walloping tails, the whales off Wales
Whack waves to wicked whitecaps,
And while they snore on their watery floor
They wear wet woolen nightcaps.

The whales! The whales! The whales off Wales,
They're always spouting fountains,
And while they glide through the tilting tide
They move like melting mountains.

Cows

The cows that browse in pastures
Seem not at all surprised
That as they moo they mow the lawn
And their milk comes pasture-ized.

Sea Horse and Sawhorse

A sea horse saw a sawhorse
On a seesaw meant for two.
"See here, sawhorse," said sea horse,
"May I seesaw with you?"

"I'll see, sea horse," said sawhorse.
"You see, I'm having fun
Seeing if I'll be seasick
On a seesaw meant for one."

Bee

You want to make some honey?
All right, here's the recipe:
Pour the juice of a thousand flowers
Through the sweet tooth of a bee.

Crocodile

The crocodile's a social sort.
In bumpy green apparel
Crocs paddle round their jungle pool
Like pickles in a barrel.

The crocodile can smile with style
And chuckle kindly, too.
Oh, he's the friendliest of beasts—
In fact, he's fond of YOU!

Lion

Who bounded headfirst from the Ark?
  Whose roar's a hurricane?
Who shakes whole jungles in the dark
  With all his might and mane?

Lion. That's who adores to roar.
  And when you're with a lion
The nearest house that has a door
  Is good to keep an eye on.

Electric Eel

Some think Electric Eel lacks looks,
But others find it stunning.
A homegrown battery it packs
To keep its shocker running.

Why, you could light all New York's streets
And skyscrapers and stuff
With one Electric Eel alone
If it were long enough.

Invisible Cat

Snow Leopard caught a wicked cough
And sneezed so hard his spots fell off.
Now every time it starts in snowing,
Don't look for him. He won't be showing.

Snail

The snail is skilled at going slow:
   It spans the earth by inches.
Where it has gone a trail will show.
   Its brave horn seldom flinches.

A dome of chalk upon its back,
   It lets a mayfly ride it
And when it wants to take a nap
   It curls itself inside it.

Yellowthroat

Sway on your cattail, Yellowthroat,
    A moment till I ask,
Why does a bird who sounds so sweet—
"Witchery witchery witchery WHEAT"—
    Wear that black robber's mask?

"Child, keep my secret from the rest
    And you shall have my thanks:
The grass with which I thatch my nest
(The long well-watered kind works best)
    I rob from river banks."

Octopus

The octopus is one tough cuss
With muscles built like truckers'.
He lifts great weights in all eight arms,
Each lined with sticky suckers.

If you should meet an octopus
Who greets you, "Hi! Let's shake!"
You'll stand a long while wondering
Which tentacle to take.

Skunk and Skink

Said the skunk to the skink,
  "Let's go sail in my skiff.
It's the one painted pink."
  Said the skink, "I'm scared stiff.

"Though I'd like to go scoot
  Over waves with you, Skunk,
If we sank, how I'd hate
  To get sick in my bunk!"

"Don't be scared," the skunk scoffed.
  "Skiffs that skim seldom sink."
So away to the skiff
  Skipped the skunk and the skink.

73

Giraffes' Laughs Last

When spied on in a zoo, Giraffe
   Neglects his tree-leaf diet
To take a look at you and laugh! —
   Your short neck! What a riot!

He grins a grin from ear to ear.
   If you've not yet departed,
In several days you'll get to hear
   The throaty laugh you started.

6

Peculiar Characters

Mechanical Menagerie

My Uncle Ike's an engineer.
He has the nutty habit
Of building beasts from wheels and wire.
He's built a robot rabbit

That hides in manholes in the street
And lives on tinfoil lettuce.
His brand new chrome-trimmed crocodile
Keeps trying hard to get us.

He has lightning bugs that come with plugs,
Electric eels that boil,
A bat that flies on batteries,
An oyster that you oil,

A forty-four-seat elephant
With a trunk so you can pack her,
And a parrot that says, "Polly want
A lighted cannon cracker!"

Stan Stapler

My friend Stan Stapler, he's the most!
  I saw his two front teeth
Bite through a stack of buttered toast
  And fold flat underneath.

A Fashion Plate

A persnickety man from Le Mans
Would wear nothing but clothes made of bronze
  Except for his socks,
  Which he'd carve out of rocks,
And a stainless steel suit of long johns.

Swept off His Pins

Mister Malachi O'Malley
Rumbled down the bowling alley
In hardly any time at all,
His thumb stuck in his bowling ball,
And landed sweetly as you like —
CRASH! BANG! BONGO! — perfect strike.

Hooked on Books

A remarkable man of Bound Brook
Likes to hang up his coat on a hook,
   But what makes him of note
   Is he keeps on his coat
While he dangles, absorbed in a book.

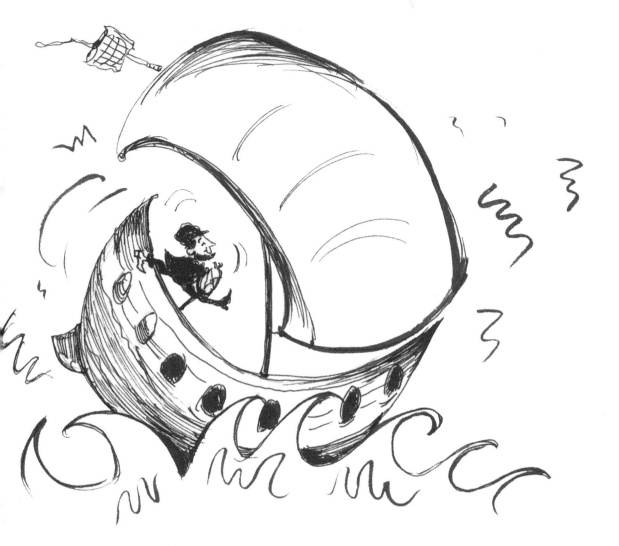

A Nervous Sea Captain
from Cheesequake

A nervous sea captain from Cheesequake
Delighted in earthquake and seasquake.
   Said he, "'Tisn't the noise
   That I truly enjoys,
It's them xylophone notes when my knees quake."

Robert Robot

Robert Robot, go unscrew
Your burnt-out head, stick in a new!

Floss your filthy teeth with wire!
Go oil your nose! Shoeshine your tire!

Don't stand there like a screw-loose dolt!
Pick up a wrench and twist your bolt!

Light your lightbulb! Look alive!
Dust your dirty old disk drive!

Stevie the Internet Addict

While staring at the Internet
Young Stevie Stoop would quite forget
To do his homework, change his socks,
Or dump his kitten's litter box.
He'd tiptoe out of bed by night
To download some remote web site
And though his best friends used to shout,
"Hey, want to play?" he'd not come out.
His poor dog begged him for a walk
But he stayed lost in keyboard talk.
One day while Stevie moved his mouse
A fire broke out, right in his house.
The firemen found him where he sat
Involved in an intensive chat
And through the thick and smoky air
They hauled him out, still in his chair.

It's nice to gaze on worlds afar,
But notice sometimes where you are.

Uncle Switch

The Man Who Does Everything Backward

Crack of dawn. Uncle Switch milks the pup,
Walks the Jersey cow, sloshes a cup
    Full of hot exercise,
    Reads two fresh eggs, and fries
All the morning news sunny-side up.

My, how well Uncle Switch fixed the clock's
Little problem! It now sits and rocks
    In his favorite chair
    While with hands in the air
Uncle points and cuckoos and ticktocks.

Uncle Switch, wearing whiskers and fur,
Is determined to practice his purr
    And solicits advice
    On how best to catch mice
From a cat he addresses as "Sir."

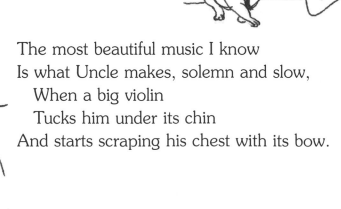

The most beautiful music I know
Is what Uncle makes, solemn and slow,
    When a big violin
    Tucks him under its chin
And starts scraping his chest with its bow.

Howland Hound can write stories and sketch,
Draw with crayons and paint, sculpt, and etch,
    And across Mucky Crick
    He keeps throwing a stick
Which he's teaching his master to fetch.

When his frog Freddy sings, Uncle croaks,
And he blubbers when told funny jokes.
    Peeling onions, he laughs,
    And he snaps photographs
Of his camera to send to its folks.

"Happy birthday, dear Uncle!" we shout.
"You have presents to give us, no doubt?"
    With a sugary *squish*
    Of cake making a wish,
All the candles blow Uncle Switch out.

What We Might Be, What We Are

If you were a scoop of vanilla
And I were the cone where you sat,
If you were a slowly pitched baseball
And I were the swing of a bat,

If you were a shiny new fishhook
And I were a bucket of worms,
If we were a pin and a pincushion,
We *might* be on intimate terms.

If you were a plate of spaghetti
And I were your piping-hot sauce,
We'd not even need to write letters
To put our affection across.

But you're just a piece of red ribbon
In the beard of a Balinese goat
And I'm a New Jersey mosquito.
I guess we'll stay slightly remote.

7

Ever Hear Tell Of . . . ?

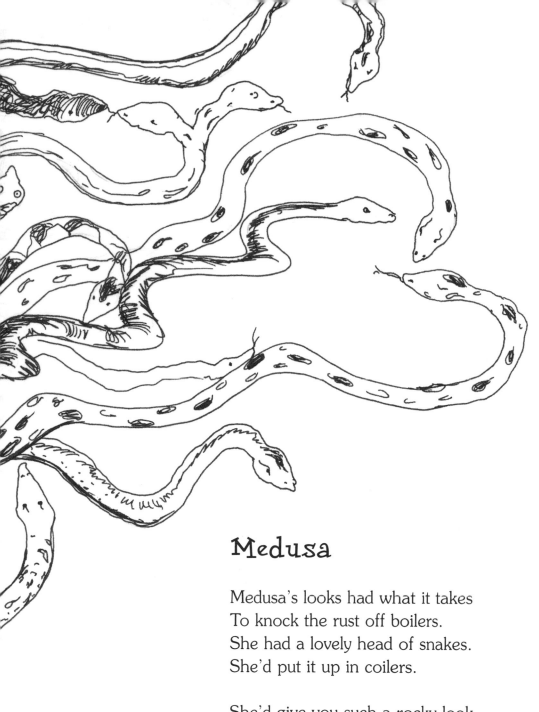

Medusa

Medusa's looks had what it takes
To knock the rust off boilers.
She had a lovely head of snakes.
She'd put it up in coilers.

She'd give you such a rocky look
Out of her old eye sockets,
You'd feel your bones all turn to stones
And pebbles fill your pockets.

King Tut

King Tut
Crossed over the Nile
On stepping-stones
Of crocodile.

"King Tut!"
His mother said,
"Come here this minute!
You'll get wet feet."
King Tut is dead

And now King Tut
Tight as a nut
Keeps his big fat Mummy shut.

King Tut,
Tut, tut.

A Visit to the Gingerbread House

"Why, sit down!" (So I let myself settle
In a fudge chair.) "I'll put on the kettle,"
  Purred the witch. "Here, just try
  Some delicious toad pie
And a cup of hot Hansel and Gretel."

Mingled Yarns

What stories are mixed together?

1 Whose cherry tree did young George chop?
    It was Pinocchio's
    And every time George told a lie
    He grew an inch of nose.

2 Jack be nimble,
    Jack be quick,
    Jack jump over
    The beanstalk stick!

3 While shepherds watched their flocks by night
  With muskets close at hand,
  An angel of the Lord came down
  And cried, "Two if by land!"

4 Aladdin had a little lamp,
  It smelled all keroseny,
  And everywhere Aladdin took
  His lamp jam-packed with genii.

  He took his lamp to school one day,
  Which made the teacher blubber
  And all the children laugh to see
  Young Al the old lamp-rubber.

Jerboa

The tale is told that when the Ark
Was hoisting anchor Noah
Cried, "Stop! What's happened to those mice
That jump?"
                    Then two jerboa
Jumped for their lives, just made the boat,
And hit the deck *thud! thud!*

Old Noah stroked his beard and smiled.
"All right now. Let it flood."

Whistler's Father

Whistler's mother — she's world famous
From a painting by her son.
What became of Whistler's father?
He's the seldom-mentioned one.

What does Whistler's father look like
Propped up in his straight-backed chair?
Does he whisper through white whiskers?
Has he wisps of whisk-broom hair?

Whistler's father, stiffly collared,
In the fussiest of coats
With his penknife, sitting whittling
Fleets of little wooden boats,

Whistling softly with his whistler
Long low whistles — can that be
Whistler's father? If I wish it,
Will he whittle one for me?

Roc

The roc, when snacks are what it wants,
  Instead of flying solo
Will carry off whole elephants.
  Who says so? Marco Polo.

And in *A Thousand and One Nights*
  You'll read how this huge condor
Can spiral up to dizzy heights
  And round the wide world wander.

Why, just to circle one roc's egg
  Took Sinbad fifty paces.
His turban tied around her leg,
  He hitchhiked to far places.

You've counted sheep? You still can't sleep?
  Try counting rocs instead,
For then, if you should chance to dream,
  You'll have rocs in your head.

8

Unlikely Doings

Two Doorbells

Two doorbells glowered out at me
With buttons big and bright.
Which one to push? Was it the left
Or the right one that was right?

I plucked up courage, pushed the right —
I pushed it good and strong —
An angry eagle came. Good night,
I must have rung dead wrong!

He shrieked, "I've flown down one whole flight
Of stairs, you runt! Pray tell,
What makes you think you've got a right
To wrong me and my bell?"

He slammed the door so hard it left
My glasses with no glass.
Well, I gave the left-hand bell a press —
Right soon, a braying ass,

A rhino with his rump on wrong,
A tribe of owls that sang
An odd, fowl-sounding sort of song,
A red orang-utang,

A mummy coming all unwrapped
And a huge blue shark replied.
The shark, his jaws wide open, snapped,
"Why don't you step inside?"

I turned toes right around and left,
Which didn't take me long.
I'd got the number right, all right,
But that street was downright wrong.

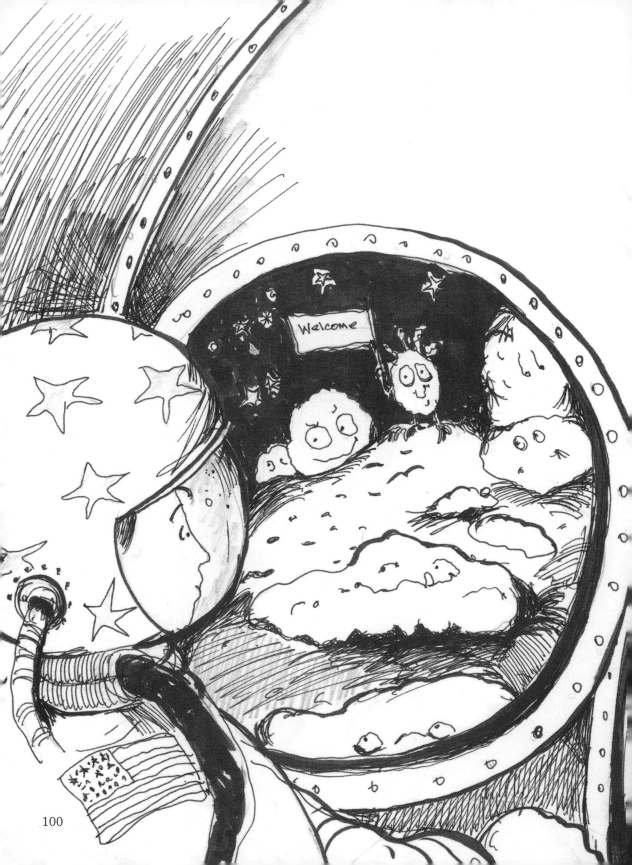

The Nineteenth-Moon-of-Neptune Beasts

Who lives on Neptune's nineteenth moon?
How are its ski conditions?
Why haven't we heard a single word
From the previous expeditions?

We skim low for a look around.
We splash down. While untwisting
Our airlock door I catch the sound
Of baby beasts insisting,

"Please, Mom, can't we eat something else?
Yes, honestly, we've *tried,*
But these screwy eggs with rockets on
Have funny bugs inside!"

Mixed-up School

We have a crazy mixed-up school.
Our teacher Mrs. Cheetah
Makes us talk backwards. Nicer cat
You wouldn't want to meet a.

To start the day we eat our lunch,
Then do some heavy dome-work.
The boys' and girls' rooms go to us,
The hamster marks our homework.

At recess time we race inside
To don our diving goggles,
Play pin-the-donkey-on-the-tail,
Ball-foot or ap-for-bobbles.

Old Cheetah with a chunk of chalk
Writes right across two blackbirds,
And when she says, "Go home!" we walk
The whole way barefoot backwards.

103

Basketball Bragging

Agatha Goop with a whale of a whoop
Swept a swisher through the hoop

And told her teammates, "There you are!
You guys are dog meat! I'm the star!"

Her teammates knew just what to do:
They dribbled her down and they dunked her through.

Now Agatha's nose may be out of joint,
But she had to admit that they'd made their point.

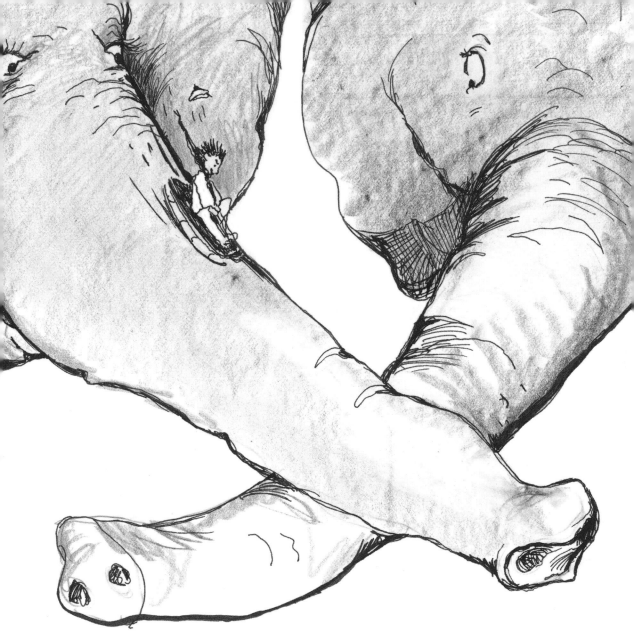

A Mammoth Roller-Coaster

Down the trunks of two elephants, Daredevil Jed
At incredible speed took a slide on his sled
And he bounced as he shot down those nose-hoses' chutes —
Blubbery brutes have such rubbery snoots.

Should All of This Come True

If combs could brush their teeth,
If a needle's eye shed tears,
If bottles craned their necks,
If corn pricked up its ears,

If triangles held their sides
And laughed, if down the street
A mile like a millipede
Ran by on wavy feet,

If cans of laundry lye
Declared they tell no fibs,
If baked potatoes dug
Umbrellas in the ribs,

If sheets of rain were starched,
If a brook, with mutterings,
Rolled over in its bed
With a deep creek of springs,

Should all of this come true
And all time were to pass,
Then you could slice a piece of cheese
With any blade of grass.

No Lie
Lye

Fairy Airline

A Tale for Saint Patrick's Day

In all Tipperary there wasn't one fairy
Who didn't feel jealous to see jumbo jets
Arise out of Shannon like shot from a cannon.
So, catching a June bug in gossamer nets,

With prodding and poking, to their seats in NON-SMOKING
Between that bug's wings all the wee folk made haste.
"Snap your belts!" yelled the pilot. "Lock the door to the
   t'ilet!" —
And that flight down a runway of firefly lights raced,

Lifted nose, did a wheelie, leaped to clouds white and mealy
Where in daylily cups Steward Harebell served dew.
Said a bowlegged rainbow, "Will you look at that plane go!"
'Twas the smoothest of flights till a wicked wind blew.

Little Biddy O'Banshee shrieked like some Comanche —
"Och, we're sure to splash down in a sea of green brine!"
Meanwhile, back at the tower ('twas a cowslip in flower)
They declared, "Some old owl must have swallowed Flight Nine!"

But their plight wasn't terrible. Copilot Clarabelle
Urged them off the bug's back with the help of her boots
And like silk from a thistle, as slick as a whistle
They unfurled their own wings and — bedad! — they had chutes!

Soon, the wind gently shifting, on down they went drifting
To a sweet field mist-glistening and buttercup-belled.
For emergency landing, sure, you'll have to be handing
First prize to the airline that's fairy-propelled.

Instant Storm

One day in Thrift-Rite Supermart
My jaw dropped wide with wonder,
For there, right next to frozen peas,
Sat frozen French-fried thunder,
Vanilla-flavored lightning bolts,
Fresh-frozen raindrop rattle —
So I bought the stuff and hauled it home,
And grabbed my copper kettle.

I'd cook me a mess of homemade storm!
But when it started melting,
The thunder shook my kitchen sink,
The ice-cold rain kept pelting,
Eight lightning bolts bounced round the room
And snapped my pancake turners —
What a crying shame!
                    Then a rainbow came
And spanned my stove's front burners.

How to Treat Shoes

Try seeing through shoes' points of view.
    Bend ear to hear your sneakers.
They've tongues to talk. At times they squawk:
    New shoes contain loud squeakers.

Suppose one day your shoes and you
    Should suddenly change places —
Then how would YOU like being two
    With feet inside your faces?

Through chewing-gum stuck to the street,
    Through snowdrifts when it's snowing,
Would you be happy hauling feet
    Wherever they were going?

Make friends with shoes. Nights when they lie,
    Tired from your daylong paces,
Be sure you feed them shoo-fly pie
    And licorice shoelaces.

Sheepshape

I shear sheep in all sorts of shapes
Like shooting stars and spangles.
I shear them in the shapes of apes.
My ewe has four right angles.

I give some sheep a camel's back,
Two mountains and a valley.
I make short shrift of them with shears.
Me, I don't shilly-shally.

I shear sheep short. Their wiry wool
Is well worthwhile to save.
Oh, what sheer joy it is to give
A shaggy sheep a shave!

One Winter Night in August

How many things are wrong with this story?

One winter night in August
While the larks sang in their eggs,
A barefoot boy with shoes on
Stood kneeling on his legs.

At ninety miles an hour
He slowly strolled downtown
And parked atop a tower
That had just fallen down.

He asked a kind old policeman
Who bit small boys in half,
"Officer, have you seen my pet
Invisible giraffe?"

"Why, sure, I haven't seen him,"
The cop smiled with a sneer.
"He was just here tomorrow
And he rushed right back next year.

"Now, boy, come be arrested
For stealing frozen steam!"
And whipping out his pistol,
That cop carved some hot ice cream.

Just then a pack of dogfish
Who roam the desert snows
Arrived by unicycle
And shook the policeman's toes.

They cried, "Congratulations,
Old dear! Surprise, surprise!
You raced the worst, so you came in first
And you didn't win any prize."

Then turning to the boyfoot bear,
They yelled, "He's overheard
What we didn't say to the officer!
We never said a word!

"Too bad, boy, we must turn you
Into a loathsome toad!
Now shut your ears and listen —
We're going to explode!"

But then, with an awful holler
That didn't make a peep,
Our ancient boy (age seven)
Woke up and went to sleep.

Index